Escape from Elephant Island

Written by **Alison Hawes**

Contents

Chapter One
Trapped!

In August 1914, Ernest Shackleton and his crew
sailed from England to Antarctica.

He was an explorer and this was his third trip there.

On this trip, he planned to walk 1,800 miles across
Antarctica.

No one had done this before.

Ernest Shackleton

By December, Shackleton's ship had almost
reached Antarctica.
But then the sea began to freeze.
At first, the wooden ship cut through the sea ice.
But the ice got thicker and thicker.

**Antarctica is covered in ice.
In some places the ice is three miles thick.**

In the end, the ice was so thick,
the ship could not go on.
But it could not go back either.
It was stuck.
They were trapped in the ice!

**Shackleton's ship, Endurance,
trapped in the sea ice.**

For nine months, Shackleton and his men lived on the ship.
The ship was locked in the ice.
The thick ice floated on the sea.
As it drifted, it took the ship with it.
It took them further away from Antarctica.

Shackleton took 27 men with him on the trip.

Endurance finally sank on November 21st 1915.

All this time, the ice was pressing against the ship.
Then, in October 1915, the ship began to break up.
Shackleton and his men took food and tools and
three lifeboats off the ship.
Then they set up camp on the ice.
In November, the ship sank.

Chapter Two
Elephant Island

Shackleton and his men camped on the ice
for five months.
Then at last the ice began to melt.
It began to crack under their feet.
Quickly, they got into the lifeboats.

Camping on the ice.

Many of the men were very ill.
They all had frostbite.
They had very little food or water left.
Shackleton had to get them to
an island as quickly as possible.

They set off in the lifeboats in April 1916.

He found a small island on his map.

It was called Elephant Island.

It was covered in snow and ice and rocks.

No one lived there, but it would have to do.

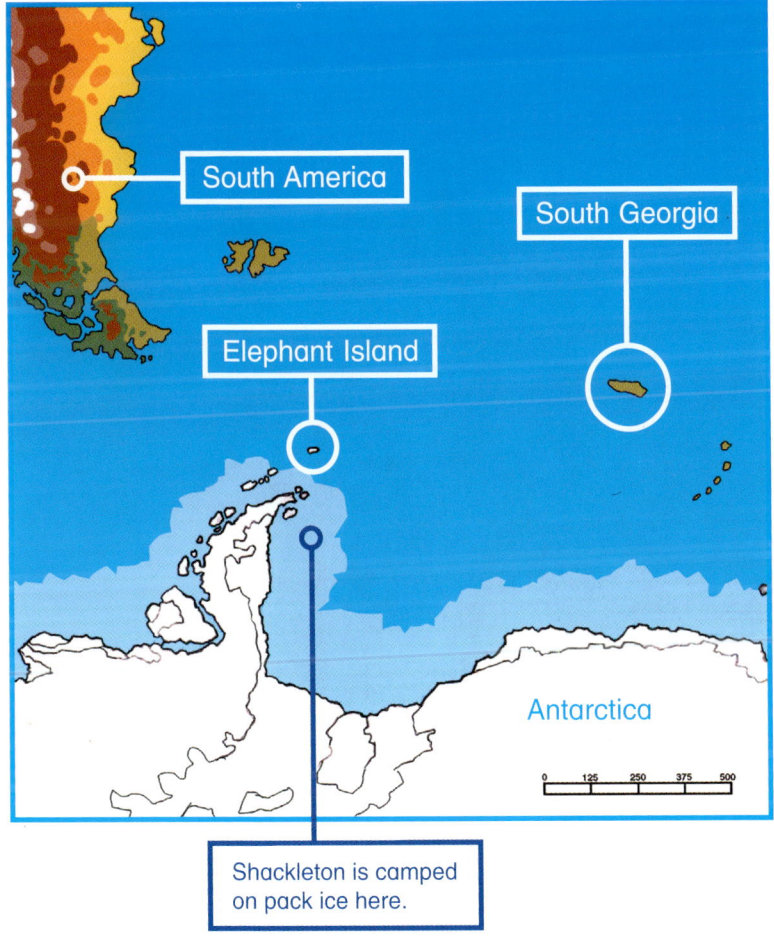

South America

South Georgia

Elephant Island

Antarctica

0   125   250   375   500

Shackleton is camped
on pack ice here.

For a week they rowed through heavy seas,
until at last they got to Elephant Island.
It was freezing cold and the wind ripped their tents.
But after months on the ice,
they were on land again!

Shackleton knew no one would come
to rescue them from Elephant Island.
No one knew where they were.
They had no radio, so they could not
call for help.

Elephant Island

Chapter Three
Help

There was just one way that Shackleton
could save his men.
He had to go and get help.
He would go to the island of South Georgia
and ask the people who lived there for help.

Shackleton explains his plan to the men.

It was a mad plan.

South Georgia was 800 miles away.

His little wooden lifeboat could sink in the stormy seas.

Or he might not find the island.

Then they would all die.

The lifeboat, the James Caird, was only 7m long.

But Shackleton went anyway!
He took five men with him.
They packed the lifeboat.
Then they waved goodbye to the other men.
They did not know if they would ever see
them again.

Their little lifeboat was tossed in the stormy seas.
They were seasick and soaked to the skin in the
icy water.
Many times they thought the lifeboat would sink.

Somehow they got there.
It took them 17 days and at last
they landed on South Georgia.
But there was no one there.

Chapter Four
Rescue

The people of South Georgia lived on the other
side of the island.
To get there, the men had to cross high mountains.
No one had ever crossed the mountains before.
So there was no map to show them the way.

South Georgia

Three of the men were too ill to cross the mountains.
Shackleton said he would send a boat to pick them up.
Shackleton and the other two men walked and
climbed for 36 hours, without sleep.
Then at last, they saw the people of South Georgia!

Shackleton told them that he had sailed from Elephant Island, to get help.

The people of South Georgia could not believe he had sailed 800 miles in a little wooden lifeboat!

Shackleton also told them about the three sick men he had left on the other side of the island.

Some of the people set off at once to rescue them.

All this time, the 22 men left on
Elephant Island waited.
They built a home out of the two boats
that had been left behind.
They ate penguin and shellfish.
They sang songs and told stories.
And they waited and hoped that
Shackleton would come back for them.

Four times, Shackleton set out on different ships,
to get to Elephant Island.
Three times, he had to go back because of the ice.
But, at last, on the fourth try, he got to the island.
His men had been on the island for four months.
Now he was taking everyone home!

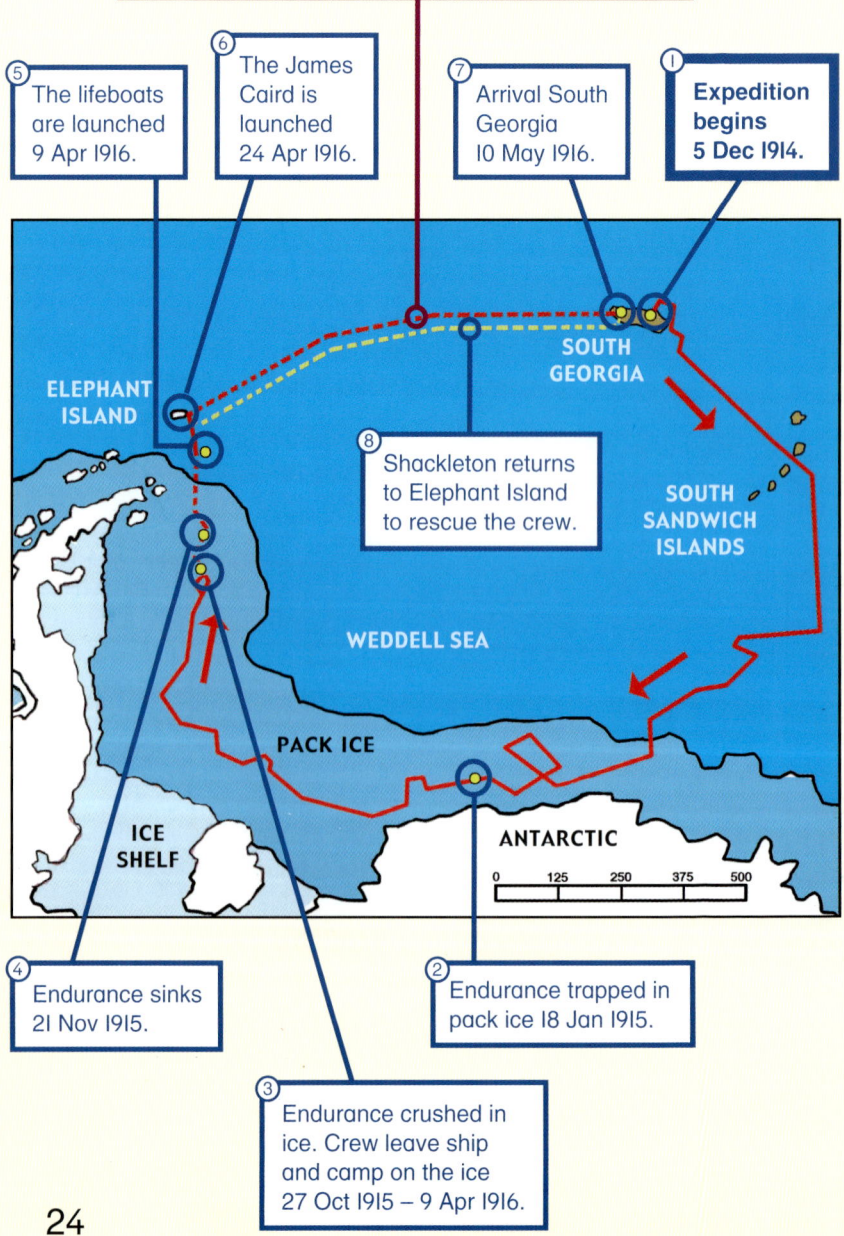

800 mile boat journey.
This is the longest sea journey ever made in a lifeboat.
(See Guinness Book of Records 2003 edition.)

⑤ The lifeboats are launched 9 Apr 1916.

⑥ The James Caird is launched 24 Apr 1916.

⑦ Arrival South Georgia 10 May 1916.

① **Expedition begins 5 Dec 1914.**

ELEPHANT ISLAND

SOUTH GEORGIA

⑧ Shackleton returns to Elephant Island to rescue the crew.

SOUTH SANDWICH ISLANDS

WEDDELL SEA

PACK ICE

ICE SHELF

ANTARCTIC

0 125 250 375 500

④ Endurance sinks 21 Nov 1915.

② Endurance trapped in pack ice 18 Jan 1915.

③ Endurance crushed in ice. Crew leave ship and camp on the ice 27 Oct 1915 – 9 Apr 1916.